Why Do Leaves Change Colour?

Rachel Griffiths

and other questions about plants

WHY IS IT SO?
?
Science

CAMBRIDGE
UNIVERSITY PRESS

Do large
seeds grow
into tall
plants?

Why do
leaves change
colour?

Contents

Questions about colour and age

Q: why do most plants have green leaves?

A: Plants have green leaves when they have **chlorophyll** in their leaves and **stems**. Chlorophyll changes the energy from sunlight into food for the plants.

Q: why do leaves change colour?

A: When the weather is cold, trees stop making chlorophyll and so the leaves are not green any more. We can see different colours in the leaves, usually yellow, orange and red.

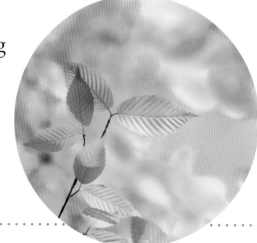

Q: Why are flowers different colours?

A: Flowers need to attract different creatures to help them to **reproduce**. Red and yellow flowers attract birds. Bees like blue flowers. Butterflies prefer flowers that are pink, purple or white.

Q: How do we know how old a tree is?

A: We can tell how old a tree is by counting the rings in its trunk. Most trees grow one growth ring each year.

Questions about plants

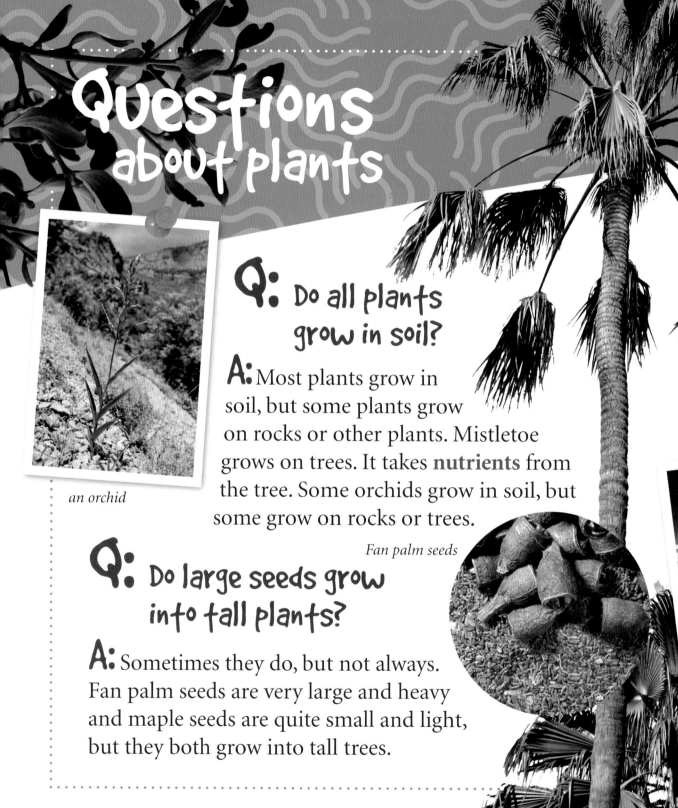

Q: Do all plants grow in soil?

A: Most plants grow in soil, but some plants grow on rocks or other plants. Mistletoe grows on trees. It takes **nutrients** from the tree. Some orchids grow in soil, but some grow on rocks or trees.

an orchid

Fan palm seeds

Q: Do large seeds grow into tall plants?

A: Sometimes they do, but not always. Fan palm seeds are very large and heavy and maple seeds are quite small and light, but they both grow into tall trees.

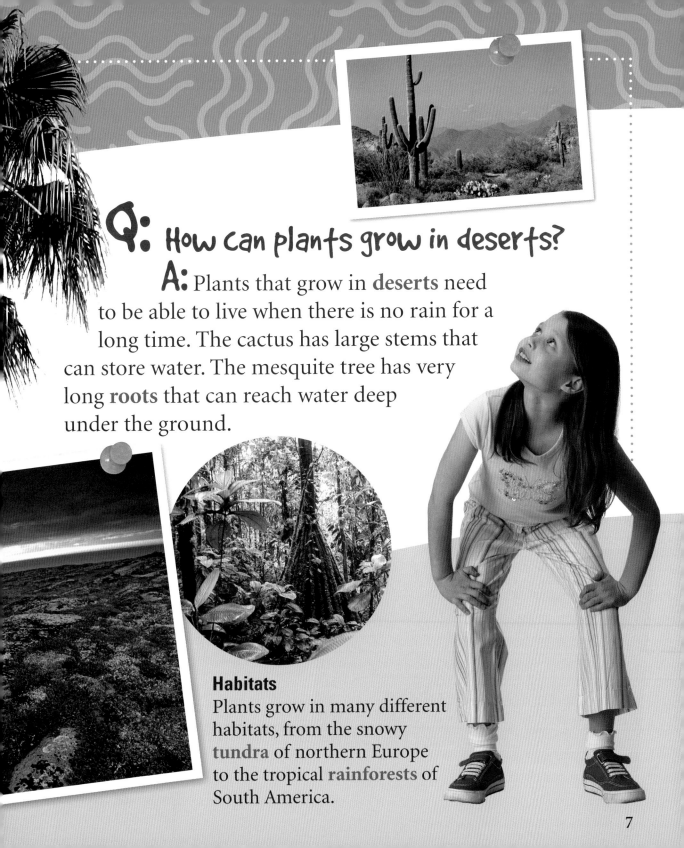

Q: How can plants grow in deserts?

A: Plants that grow in **deserts** need to be able to live when there is no rain for a long time. The cactus has large stems that can store water. The mesquite tree has very long **roots** that can reach water deep under the ground.

Habitats
Plants grow in many different habitats, from the snowy **tundra** of northern Europe to the tropical **rainforests** of South America.

It's a fact

California's giant redwood

> Red leaves

Visiting places when the leaves turn red in Autumn is a tradition called Momijigari in Japan. Many people go to see the beautiful maple trees near Kyoto.

> Tallest tree in the world

The tallest tree in the world is a giant redwood called Hyperion. It is 115.5 metres (m) tall and grows in the Redwood National Park on the north-west coast of the USA.

autumn maples in Japan

Baobab

> Tallest tree ever

The tallest tree ever measured was a Douglas fir tree in Canada. In the 1890s it was 126 m tall.

> The Baobab tree

This South African tree is not very tall, but it is extremely fat. It can grow twice as wide as it is tall.

coolibah tree

> Plants for health

People have used plants to make medicines for thousands of years. The ancient Egyptians made medicines from garlic, coriander and mint. Native Americans used the Californian poppy for toothache and some Aboriginal Australians used the sap from the coolibah tree for snake bites.

garlic

Californian poppy

Can you believe it?

the Rafflesia flower

AmazingR afflesia

The Rafflesia flower is the largest flower in the world. It has no stems, roots or leaves and it smells like bad meat.

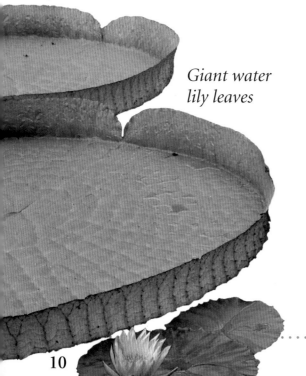

Giant water lily leaves

Fast-growing bamboo

Bamboo is the fastest-growing plant in the world. It can reach its full size in only four years.

A giant water lily

The leaves of this giant water lily are very strong. A child can stand on them.

Old as Methuselah

A bristlecone pine, called Methuselah, is the oldest known living tree in the world. This tree is more than 4,000 years old.

King Clone

A creosote bush in the Mojave Desert in the USA is older than Methuselah. It is called King Clone and people think it is nearly 12,000 years old.

Snap!

Many animals eat plants, but did you know that some plants eat animals?
The Venus fly trap snaps shut on insects that touch the little hairs on its leaves. Then the plant eats the insect.

Venus fly trap

Who found out?

Botanist: Carl Linnaeus

Carl Linnaeus (1707–1778) was a Swedish professor who listed, grouped and named thousands of plants and animals. All over the world **botanists** now use Linnaeus's system for naming plants so that although they speak many different languages they still use the same names for plants and animals. Linnaeus was also a great teacher who taught many botanists.

Collector of plants: Joseph Banks

Sir Joseph Banks (1743–1820) was an English botanist who joined Captain Cook's 1768 expedition to Tahiti. He collected plants in South America, Tahiti and New Zealand before reaching Australia in 1770. In Australia Sir Joseph Banks collected more than 110 previously unknown plants.

Age of trees:
Andrew Ellicott Douglass

Andrew Douglass (1867–1962) was an American scientist who studied tree rings in trees and in **timber** in old buildings. He noted that in dry years tree rings were thin. He compared the patterns of tree rings to work out the year that a tree was cut down.

the banksia flower, named after Joseph Banks

It's quiz time!

1 Draw lines to match the questions and answers.

1. Who discovered how to work out the ages of trees?

2. Why do most plants have green leaves?

3. Why do leaves change colour?

4. Why are flowers different colours?

5. How do we know how old a tree is?

a) By counting the rings in its trunk.

b) Andrew Douglass, who was an American scientist.

c) So they can attract different creatures to help them reproduce.

d) Because chlorophyll makes them green.

e) Because plants stop making chlorophyll when it is cold.

2 Can you find the hidden plant words?

aksntodkgleaveskgjthstemlkjtrootsoejtntrunkdmenchlorophyll
msjehntseedshdieflower

3 Solve the crossword.

Across:

1. It has a large stem to store water
3. It smells like bad meat
6. Bees like this colour flower

Down:

2. The Baobab tree is very fat but not very _ _ _ _
3. We count them to tell how old the tree is
4. We plant seeds in _ _ _ _
5. It is the tallest tree in the world

4 Choose the correct words.

1. Chlorophyll changes the energy from sunlight into (food / water / air) for the plants.

2. We can tell how old a tree is by counting the (rings / bracelets / holes) in its trunk.

3. People make (metal / medicines / meat) from plants.

4. The Venus fly trap eats (plants / children / insects).

Glossary

botanist: scientist who studies plants

chlorophyll: the substance in leaves that gives them their green colour

desert: hot, dry land where few plants can grow

nutrients: types of food plants or animals need to grow

rainforest: dense forest with a lot of rain, usually in the tropics

reproduce: to make new, baby versions of an animal or plant

roots: underground part of a plant

stem: the main stalk of the plant which leaves and flowers grow from

timber: large pieces of wood used in a building

tundra: the flat lands in the cold, northern parts of the world where trees do not grow